Easy CSS - Handy Guide

Discover the World of the Web Programming

INDEX

Animations

Responsive design

Optimization of the CSS code

Browser compatibility and fallback

Framework CSS

Intro

Welcome to "Easy CSS - Handy Guide". This book will take you on an exciting journey to discover CSS by offering you a perfect combination of theory and practice. We'll explore the fundamentals of CSS by learning how to select elements and create responsive layouts that adapt to different screen sizes. We'll also delve into the art of applying creative text styles, glamorous backgrounds, and elegant borders to bring your digital creations to life.

But it doesn't end there! We will also guide you through the world of CSS animations, transformations and transitions, to add movement and dynamism to your designs. You will understand how to optimize your CSS code, improving performance and ensuring smooth navigation for users.

With "Easy CSS - Handy Guide" in your hands, you'll have everything you need to become a CSS expert and to create mind-blowing designs. Whether you're a beginner or an expert, this guide will be your trusted companion along the way, giving you in-depth knowledge and lots of creative ideas to put into practice. Get ready to immerse yourself in a universe of possibilities and turn your visions into breathtaking digital realities.

Have fun!

Development environment

Introduction

This manual includes a dedicated development environment, which means it avoids the need to set up a local development environment, which can vary from computer to computer. Using the included development environment is more convenient and faster, as no software installation is required. Furthermore, it will be possible to test written pages directly from the browser.

Configuration

To access the dedicated development environment, connect to the site https://easy-code.cloud/board .
After registering or logging in, you will immediately find the development environment ready for use.

To create a new page click on the 'add' button in the left side column. Enter a name for the page respecting the constraints, choose the desired language from the drop-down menu and finally press 'Create'. You will find the summary of all the pages you have created in the left side column.

To write on a page, click on its name: the text editor will open, allowing you to write code on it.

Introduction to CSS

What is CSS?

CSS, acronym for Cascading Style Sheets, is a style language used to define the visual appearance of an HTML document. In other words, CSS allows us to make our website or HTML page aesthetically appealing and well structured.

Imagine having an HTML document as a basic structure that defines the arrangement of contents: titles, paragraphs, images, links and so on. However, without CSS, our document would just be a simple collection of text without any formatting or styling.

This is where CSS comes into play. It allows us to create rules that specify how we want HTML elements to appear on the screen. We can define text color, font type, margin, padding, size and position of elements, background color and many other stylistic aspects.

The great strength of CSS is that its styles can be applied selectively. We can create CSS rules that apply only to certain elements or groups of elements, allowing us to customize the look to suit our needs. Furthermore, CSS is designed with a cascading system, which means that rules can be overridden or inherited based on the specificity of the selector and the position of the declarations within the document.

CSS offers a wide range of functionality that goes beyond just formatting text. We can create complex layouts, animations, transitions, visual effects and much more. It is a powerful language that allows developers to transform a simple HTML document into an engaging and captivating visual presentation.

CSS syntax

The basic syntax of CSS is essential for defining styling rules and applying them to HTML elements. Here is an overview of the CSS syntax:

- **Selector**: The selector identifies the HTML elements you want to style. You can use different types of selectors, such as tag selectors, class selectors, ID selectors, attribute selectors, and combination selectors.

- **Declaration block**: The declaration block is enclosed in braces {}. Contains the properties and their values that define the style to be applied to the selected elements.

- **Declaration**: A declaration consists of a property followed by a colon (:) and a value. For example, "color: blue;" defines the "color" property with the value "blue", which sets the text color to blue.

- **Property**: Properties define the specific aspects of the elements you want to change. For example, "font-size" defines the font size, "background-color" sets the background color, and "margin" determines the margin around the element.

- **Values**: Values specify how the properties should be displayed. For example, the values for the "color" property might be "red", "rgb(255, 0, 0)", or "#FF0000", depending on the color system used.

- **Comments**: Comments in CSS start with "/" and end with "/". Comments are used to insert notes or explanations into the code and do not affect the final output.

Here's an example of how CSS syntax is used to define a style rule:

```
selector {
  property: value;
}
```

For example, to apply a red color to the text of all paragraph elements (<p> tags) in your HTML document, you could use the following CSS rule:

```
p {
  color: red;
}
```

Linking CSS to an HTML document

To link a CSS file to an HTML document, you can use the <link> element in the header of your HTML file. Here are the steps to follow:

- Create a Separate CSS File: First, create a separate CSS file with the ".css" extension containing the styling rules you want to apply to your HTML document. Save the CSS file with a meaningful name, such as "styles.css".

- Link the CSS file to the HTML using the <link> element: Within the header of your HTML document, insert the <link> element between the <head> and </head> tags. The <link> element is used to establish a connection between your HTML document and the external CSS file.

```
<!DOCTYPE html>
<html>
<head>
 <link rel="stylesheet" href="styles.css">
</head>
<body>
 <!-- Content of your HTML document -->
</body>
</html>
```

- Specify the path to the CSS file in the <link> tag: In the "href" attribute of the <link> element, specify the correct path to your CSS file. If your CSS file is in the same directory as your HTML file, you can simply specify the filename like in the example above. If your CSS file is in a subdirectory, specify the correct relative path, such as "css/styles.css".

Once linked successfully, your HTML document will apply the style rules defined in the external CSS file. Make sure the path to the CSS file is correct and both files are accessible from the server or from your local development environment.

Linking CSS in this way allows you to separate HTML document structure from styling, making it easier to manage and maintain your styles. You can also link multiple CSS files to your HTML document if needed, allowing for greater modularity and flexibility in developing your website.

Select elements with CSS

Basic selectors

Basic selectors in CSS allow you to select the HTML elements you want to style. Here are some examples of basic selectors:

- **Tag selector**: Select all items matching the specified type. For example, the *p* selector selects all <p> elements in the document.

- **Class selector**: Select elements that have a specified class attribute. Use the dot "." followed by the class name. For example, the *.my-class* selector selects all elements with the class "my-class".

- **ID selector**: Select the element that has a specified id attribute. Use the pound sign "#" followed by the ID name. For example, the *#my-id* selector selects the item with the ID "my-id".

- **Universal selector**: Select all elements in the document. Use the asterisk "*". For example, the selector * selects all HTML elements.

- **Attribute selector**: Select elements that have a specific attribute. Use the square brackets "[attribute=value]". For example, the *[type="text"]* selector selects elements with the type attribute equal to "text".

- **Combined selector**: Combine multiple selectors to select specific items based on combined rules. For example, the *div* selector *p* selects all <p> elements that are direct descendants of a <div> element.

By combining selectors, you can more specifically select the elements you want to apply custom styles.

Advanced selectors

In addition to basic selectors, CSS also offers advanced selectors that allow you to select elements more specifically and precisely. Here are some examples of advanced selectors:

- **Descendant selector**: Allows you to select child elements within another element. Use a space between selectors. For example, the div selector p selects all <p> elements that are direct descendants of a <div> element.

- **Direct child selector**: Select elements that are direct children of another element. Use the ">" symbol between the selectors. For example, the div > p selector only selects <p> elements that are direct children of a <div> element.

- **Advanced attribute selector**: Allows you to select elements based on specific conditions on the attributes. Some examples of advanced attribute selectors are:

  [attribute^="value"]: Select elements that have an attribute starting with the specified value.
  [attribute$="value"]: Select elements that have an attribute ending with the specified value.

[attribute*="value"]: Select elements that have an attribute that contains the specified value.

- **Pseudo-class selector**: Allows you to select items based on a particular status or location within the document. Some examples of pseudo-classes are:

  :hover: Select items when hovered with the cursor.
  :nth-child(n): Select the element which is the nth child of its parent.
  :first-child: Select the first child element of its parent.

- **Pseudo-element selector**: Allows you to select specific parts of an item, such as the first letter of a paragraph or the last item in a list. Some examples of pseudo-elements are:

  ::first-letter: Select the first letter of an element.
  ::before: Inserts content before the content of an element.
  ::after: Inserts content after the content of an element.

The combination of basic selectors and advanced selectors gives you greater flexibility and precision in selecting elements to apply specific styles to. Experiment with these selectors to get complete control over the look of your HTML document.

Pseudoselectors

Pseudo-selectors in CSS allow you to select elements based on a specific state or a particular condition. These pseudoselectors are added to selectors to extend their functionality. Here are some examples of common pseudoselectors:

- **:hover**: Select items when they are pointed at with the cursor. For example, a:hover will select all links when the cursor is over them.

- **:active**: Select items during the moment they are activated, such as when a button is pressed. For example, button:active will select all buttons when they are activated.

- **:focus**: Select the element that has active focus, for example when an input field is selected. For example, input:focus will select all input fields that have focus.

- **:first-child**: Select the first child element of its parent. For example, li:first-child will select the first <li> element in a list.

- **:last-child**: Select the last child element of its parent. For example, div:last-child will select the last <div> element within its parent.

- **:nth-child(n)**: Select the element which is the nth child of its parent. You can specify an exact number (for example :nth-child(3)) or a more complex formula using the n and even/odd expressions to select specific items based on their position.

- **:not(selector)**: Select items that do not match the specified selector. For example, :not(.class) will select all elements that don't have the specified class.

These are just a few examples of pseudoselectors available in CSS. Each pseudoselector has a specific use and can be combined with other selectors to achieve greater precision in selecting elements.

Selector combiners

Selector combiners in CSS allow you to select elements based on their relationship to other elements in the HTML document. These combinators are used to combine multiple selectors and define more complex selection rules. Here are some examples of selector combinators:

- **Descendant selector (space)**: Select child elements that are descendants of another element. For example, div p will select all <p> elements that are direct descendants of a <div> element.

- **Direct child selector (>)**: Select elements that are direct children of another element. For example, ul > li will select all <li> elements that are direct children of a <ul> element.

- **Adjacency selector (+)**: Select the first item that immediately follows another item. For example, h1 + p will select the first <p> element that immediately follows an <h1> element.

- **Generation selector (~)**: Select items that follow another item, even if not immediately. For example, ul ~ p will match all <p> elements following a <ul> element.

- **Group selector (,)**: Select several selectors separated by commas. For example, h1, h2, h3 will select all <h1>, <h2> and <h3> elements.

These selector combinators can be combined with each other to create more specific select rules. For example, div ul > li will select <li> elements that are direct children of a <ul> element which is itself a direct descendant of a <div> element.

Box model and positioning

Box model

The box model in CSS is a fundamental concept that describes how HTML elements are represented as rectangular boxes in the page layout. Each element is treated as a box made up of four main components: the content box, the padding box, the border box and the margin box.

- **Content Box**: This is the inside of the box and is where the content of the element is displayed, such as text, images or other HTML elements. The size of the content box is determined by the width and height properties.

- **Padding Box**: It is located around the content box and represents the empty space between the content and the border of the element. You can set the size of the padding using the padding-top, padding-right, padding-bottom and padding-left properties. The padding does not affect the total size of the element.

- **Border Box**: It is located around the padding box and represents the border of the element. You can set the style, color and thickness of the border using the border property. It is important to note that the border is included in the total size of the item.

- **Margin Box**: It is located around the border box and represents the empty space between the current element and the other surrounding elements. You can set the size of the margin using the margin-top, margin-right, margin-bottom and margin-left properties. The margin affects the arrangement of elements on the page.

In summary, the box model defines how the total size of an HTML element is calculated, including the content, padding, border and margin. Understanding the box model is essential for controlling the layout and positioning of elements in your HTML document using CSS.

Dimensions and units of measure

In the CSS box model, element sizes are defined using units of measurement. There are several units of measurement available in CSS. Here are some of the most common:

- **Pixel (px)**: It is the most common unit of measure used to define precise dimensions. A pixel corresponds to a single point on the screen. For example, width: 200px; sets the width of an element to 200 pixels.

- **Percentage (%)**: Percentages allow you to define the size based on a percentage of the parent or container size. For example, width: 50%; sets the width of an element to 50% of its parent's width.

- **Em (em)**: The em is a relative unit of measurement based on the font size of the parent element. For example, font-size: 1.2em; sets the font size of an element to 1.2 times the font size of the parent element.

- **Rem (rem)**: The rem is a relative unit of measurement based on the font size of the root element (usually the <html> element). Unlike em, rem does not depend on the hierarchical context. For example, font-size: 1.2rem; sets the font size of an element to 1.2 times the font size of the root element.

- **Viewport-relative units**: Viewport-related units, such as vw (viewport width) and vh (viewport height), allow you to define the size based on the size of the browser window. For example, width: 50vw; sets the width of an element to 50% of the browser window width.

- **Units of measurement related to text**: Some units of measurement are based on font size, such as ex (x-height of the font) and ch (width of the "0" font). These units can be useful for calculating text-based sizes.

It is important to choose the appropriate units of measure based on your layout and design needs. Relative units, such as percentages and ems, can be useful for creating smooth, responsive layouts. Absolute units, such as pixels, are often used for precise dimensions or when detailed layout control is required. Remember that it is possible to combine different units of measurement to get the desired result.

Positioning

There are several types of positioning you can use to control the position of elements within the page layout. Here is an explanation of the four most common placement types:

- **Positioning static**: This is the default placement type for items. Elements with static placement follow the normal flow of the document and are placed in their default position. You cannot move or stack elements with static placement using placement properties.

- **Positioning relative**: Elements with relative positioning are positioned relative to their normal position in the document flow. You can move an element with relative positioning using the top, right, bottom and left properties. These properties determine the relative displacement from the normal position of the element. Relatively positioned elements still retain their original space in the layout, even when moved.

- **Positioning absolute**: Items with absolute positioning are positioned relative to the closest container with relative, absolute, or fixed positioning. You can move an element with absolute positioning using the top, right, bottom and left properties. These properties determine the absolute displacement with respect to the placed container. Elements with absolute positioning are removed from the normal flow of the document and can overlap other elements.

- **Positioning fixed**: Items with fixed placement are placed relative to the browser window. They keep their fixed position even when scrolling the page. You can move a fixed-positioned element using the top, right, bottom, and left properties. Fixed-positioned elements are removed from the normal flow of the document and can overlap other elements.

These placement types give you finer control over the position of elements within the layout. You can use relative, absolute, and fixed positioning to create complex layouts, overlays, and specifically positioned elements.

Float and clear

In CSS, the float and clear properties are used to control the arrangement and interaction of elements within a layout. Here is an explanation of these two properties:

- **Float**: The float property allows you to move an element to the left or right with respect to the normal flow of the document. When an element is set to float: left or float: right, subsequent elements in the document flow will wrap around it. This technique is commonly used to create multi-column layouts or place images to the left or right of text. It is important to note that floated elements lose their effective height, which can affect the arrangement of subsequent elements. To avoid this problem, it is often necessary to use the clear property.

- **Clear**: The clear property is used to handle the interaction of elements with floats. When an element is set to clear: left, clear: right, or clear: both, it indicates that it should not be placed next to corresponding float elements. In practice, clear cleans up the floating area and prevents subsequent elements from wrapping around other floated elements. You can use clear on an element to place it below all previous float elements.

For example, suppose you have two floated <div> elements: one on the left and one on the right. Subsequent elements in the document flow will wrap around these float elements. To position a new element below both floats, you can apply clear: both to the next element.

Here is an example of using the float and clear properties:

```css
.float-left {
  float: left;
}

.float-right {
  float: right;
}

.clear-both {
  clear: both;
}
```

```html
<div class="float-left">Element floated to the left</div>
<div class="float-right">Element floated to the right</div>
<div class="clear-both">Next item with clear both</div>
```

In this example, the next element is placed below both float elements.

It is important to note that excessive use of floats can complicate the layout and cause alignment problems. In recent years, the use of floats has been replaced by other positioning and layout techniques, such as Flexbox and CSS Grid. However, understanding float and clear can still be useful for understanding and working with older CSS code or specific situations.

Flexbox

Basic concepts of Flexbox

Flexbox is a CSS module that provides a flexible layout system for organizing elements within a container. With Flexbox, you can control the placement, alignment and size of elements easily and efficiently.

To use Flexbox, you need to create a flex container by applying the property **display: flex;** to the container. This causes direct child items of the container to become flex items, called flex items.

Once the container is configured as a flex container, you can use the Flexbox properties to control the behavior of flex items. Some of the basic concepts of Flexbox include:

-   **Principal axis and cross axis**: Flexbox defines a principal axis and a cross axis. The primary axis is the direction along which flex items are placed within the flex container. The transverse axis is perpendicular to the principal axis. You can specify the orientation of the principal axis using the flex-direction property.

-   **Flex properties**: The flex property is used to control the size and flexibility of flex items. It is made up of three values: flex-grow, flex-shrink and flex-basis. These values determine how the flex items expand, contract, and occupy the space inside the flex container.

-   **Alignment**: Flexbox offers a number of properties for aligning items within the flex container. Some of these properties include justify-content to align along the major axis and align-items to align along the cross axis. You can also use the align-self property to control the alignment of a single flex item.

-   **Spacing**: You can control the spacing between flex items by using the justify-content property to align items along the primary axis and the align-content property to distribute the space along the cross axis.

Horizontal and vertical layout

With Flexbox, you can easily create horizontal and vertical layouts for items inside a flex container. Here's how you can do both types of layouts:

Horizontal layout:
To create a horizontal layout, set the flex container's flex-direction property to row. This way, the child elements will be placed in a horizontal row inside the container. You can use other alignment properties such as justify-content to distribute items along the main axis and align-items to align items along the cross axis. For example:

```
.container {
  display: flex;
  flex-direction: row;
  justify-content: space-between;
  align-items: center;
}
```

Vertical layout:

To create a vertical layout, set the flex container's flex-direction property to column. This way, the child elements will be placed in a vertical column inside the container. You can use alignment properties such as justify-content to distribute items along the main axis and align-items to align items along the cross axis. For example:

```
.container {
  display: flex;
  flex-direction: column;
  justify-content: center;
  align-items: flex-start;
}
```

In both examples, the .container class represents the flexible container that contains the items to be placed.

Alignment and spacing

You can control the alignment and spacing of elements within a flex container using several properties. Here are some of the most common properties for managing alignment and spacing with Flexbox:

- **justify-content**: This property is used to align items along the main axis of the flex container. You can use values such as flex-start to align items at the beginning, flex-end to align items at the end, center to align items in the middle, space-between to distribute them evenly with spacing between items, and space-around to distribute the elements with spacing both between and around elements.

- **align-items**: This property is used to align items along the cross axis of the flex container. You can use values such as flex-start to align elements to the beginning, flex-end to align elements to the end, center to align elements to the center, baseline to align them to the baseline of the text, and stretch to extend elements to fill everything the space available vertically.

- **align-self**: This property is used to override the alignment defined by align-items for a single item. You can use the same align-items values to align a specific item differently from other items in the flex container.

- **align-content**: This property is used to distribute the extra space along the cross axis when there are multiple rows of items inside the flex container. You can use values such as flex-start to align lines at the beginning, flex-end to align lines at the end, center to align lines in the middle, space-between to distribute lines evenly with spacing between them, and space-around for distribute the lines with spacing both between and around the lines.

- **gap** (or row-gap and column-gap): This property is used to specify the spacing between items within the flexible container. You can use a numeric value or a unit value to define the space between elements along the main axis and the cross axis. This property is a simpler way to manage the spacing between elements than the margin property.

Sorting and resizing

You can control the sorting and resizing of items within a flex container using some specific properties. Here are two of the main properties to handle sorting and resizing with Flexbox.

order: The order property is used to specify the display order of items within the flexible container. By default, all elements have an order value of 0, but you can use positive or negative values to change their order. Items with lower order values are displayed before those with higher order values. For example:

```
.item {
  order: 1; /* Display item as second */
}

.another-item {
  order: -1; /* Display element as first */
}
```

flex-grow and **flex-shrink**: These properties are used to control how items expand or contract to fill the available space within the flex container. The flex-grow property determines how much extra space an element can take up compared to other elements. A larger flex-grow value indicates that the element will expand more. On the other hand, the flex-shrink property indicates how much an element can shrink when there is a lack of space. For example:

```
.item {
  flex-grow: 1; /* Element expands to fill extra space */
}

.another-item {
  flex-shrink: 0; /* Item doesn't shrink when running out of space */
}
```

Using these properties, you can change the display order of items and control how they resize within the flexible container. This allows you to create dynamic and responsive layouts where elements adapt according to the available space and your viewing preferences.

CSS Grid

Basic concepts of CSS Grid

CSS Grid is a CSS layout module that allows you to create advanced and complex layouts within a web page. It's a two-dimensional grid system that allows you to place items in rows and columns.

Unlike Flexbox, which mainly focuses on arranging elements along one axis (horizontal or vertical), CSS Grid offers more precise and flexible control over arranging elements in both directions.

Here are some of the basic concepts of CSS Grid:

- **Grid container**: To create a grid with CSS Grid, you need to define a grid container using the display property with the value grid. The grid container becomes the parent of the elements that will be placed inside the grid.

- **Rows and columns**: You can specify the rows and columns within the grid container using the grid-template-rows and grid-template-columns properties. These properties allow you to define the size and arrangement of rows and columns, respectively. You can use units of measurement such as pixels, percentages, or fr, which represent a fraction of the available space.

- **Positioning of elements**: Elements within the grid are positioned using the grid-row and grid-column properties. You can specify the row or column number to place the element in, or use line names, such as start and end, to indicate row and column ends.

- **Spacing and alignment**: You can control the spacing between rows and columns using the grid-gap property. This property allows you to specify the distance between elements within the grid. You can also use the justify-items and align-items properties to align items within grid cells.

- **Implicit and explicit grids**: CSS Grid allows you to create both explicit grids, where rows and columns are explicitly specified, and implicit grids, where rows and columns are automatically created based on the contents. This offers great flexibility in defining dynamic layouts.

With CSS Grid, you can create complex and customized layouts, adapting them to your specific design needs. The combination of rows, columns, and element placement gives you precise control over the layout structure.

Creating a grid

To create a grid with CSS Grid, you need to follow a few basic steps. Here's how you can create a basic grid using CSS Grid:

Define the grid container: Start by defining a grid container using the display property with the value grid. This makes your parent element a grid.

```
.container {
  display: grid;
```

```
}
```

Specify the columns: Use the grid-template-columns property to define the columns of the grid. You can specify column sizes using units of measurement such as pixels, percentages, or fr (fractions) which represent a fraction of the available space.

```
.container {
  display: grid;
  grid-template-columns: 1fr 1fr 1fr; /* Three columns with equal width */
}
```

Specify the lines: Use the grid-template-rows property to define the rows of the grid. As with columns, you can specify the size of rows using any desired units of measure.

```
.container {
  display: grid;
  grid-template-columns: 1fr 1fr 1fr; /* Three columns with equal width */
  grid-template-rows: 100px 200px; /* Two lines with specific heights */
}
```

Place the elements within the grid: You can position elements within the grid using the grid-row and grid-column properties. You can specify the row or column number to place the element in, or use line names, such as start and end, to indicate row and column ends.

```
.container {
  display: grid;
  grid-template-columns: 1fr 1fr 1fr; /* Three columns with equal width */
  grid-template-rows: 100px 200px; /* Two lines with specific heights */
}

.item {
  grid row: 1 / 2; /* Element extends from line 1 to line 2 */
  grid column: 2 / 4; /* Element extends from column 2 to column 4 */
}
```

Add items to the grid: Add the desired items inside the grid container. Make sure you give them an appropriate class or selector to be able to apply the placement rules.

```
<div class="container">
  <div class="item">Item 1</div>
  <div class="item">Item 2</div>
  <div class="item">Item 3</div>
</div>
```

```
.container {
```

```
  display: grid;
  grid-template-columns: 1fr 1fr 1fr;
  grid-template-rows: 100px 200px;
}

.item {
  grid-row: 1 / 2;
  grid-column: 2 / 4;
}
```

These are the basic steps to create a grid using CSS Grid. You can further customize the grid using other CSS Grid properties, such as grid-gap for cell spacing, or take advantage of CSS Grid's advanced features to create more complex layouts.

Positioning of elements in the grid

Positioning of elements within a CSS Grid can be managed using several properties and values. Here are some basic concepts for positioning elements:

grid-row and **grid-column**: These properties specify the placement of an element within the grid in terms of rows and columns. You can use numbers to indicate the number of rows or columns the element spans, or you can use line names to specify the ends of the rows or columns.

```
.item {
  grid row: 1 / 3; /* Element extends from line 1 to line 2 */
  grid column: 2 / 4; /* Element extends from column 2 to column 3 */
}
```

grid-area: This property allows you to simultaneously specify the placement of an element in terms of rows and columns using an area name. You can define custom areas in the grid container using the grid-template-areas property, and then assign these areas to elements using grid-area.

```
.container {
  display: grid;
  grid-template-areas:
    "header header"
    "sidebar content"
    "footer footer";
}

.header {
  grid-area: header;
}

.sidebar {
  grid-area: sidebar;
```

```
}

.content {
  grid-area: content;
}

.footer {
  grid-area: footer;
}
```

justify-self and **align-self**: These properties allow you to align a single element within its grid cell. justify-self controls alignment along the horizontal axis, while align-self controls alignment along the vertical axis.

```
.item {
  justify-self: center; /* Align element horizontally in the center of the cell */
  align-self: end; /* Align element vertically to bottom of cell */
}
```

Responsive layout with CSS Grid

CSS Grid is a powerful tool for creating responsive layouts. It can be used to adjust the placement of elements according to screen sizes or different device views.

Use media queries: Media queries allow you to apply specific CSS rules based on screen size. You can define different grid layouts for different screen sizes within your media queries.

```
.container {
  display: grid;
  grid-template-columns: 1fr 1fr;
}

@media (max-width: 768px) {
  .container {
    grid-template-columns: 1fr;
  }
}
```

In this example, we have a two column grid layout for larger screens and switch to a single column when the screen width becomes less than 768px.

Use the grid-template-areas property: You can use grid-template-areas to define different layout configurations for different screen sizes. Assign different area names to grid cells and use media queries to change area configurations.

```
.container {
```

```
  display: grid;
  grid-template-areas:
    "header header"
    "sidebar content"
    "footer footer";
}

@media (max-width: 768px) {
  .container {
    grid-template-areas:
      "header"
      "content"
      "sidebar"
      "footer";
  }
}
```

In this example, we have a four area layout for larger screens and switch to a one column layout for smaller screens.

Use the grid-auto-flow property: The grid-auto-flow property defines how items are placed in the grid when not explicitly specified. You can use the dense value to shrink items into empty spaces within the grid.

```
.container {
  display: grid;
  grid-template-columns: repeat(auto-fit, minmax(200px, 1fr));
  grid-auto-rows: 200px;
  grid-auto-flow: dense;
}
```

In this example, we have a flexible grid layout that adjusts to the screen size. Items will automatically fit into the available columns and will be packed into blanks when needed.

Font families and typography

Using font families

Using character families (fonts) in CSS allows you to define which fonts you want to use for text within an HTML document.

Use a basic font family: You can specify a generic font family such as "serif", "sans-serif" or "monospace" for the text of your document. These font families are available on most operating systems and offer good compatibility.

```
body {
  font-family: Arial, sans-serif;
}
```

In this example, document text will be displayed in Arial font if available, otherwise a default sans-serif font will be used.

Use a specific font family: You can specify a specific font family you want to use, such as "Helvetica", "Times New Roman" or "Verdana". Be sure to include fallback alternatives in case the specific font is not available on all devices.

```
h1 {
  font-family: "Helvetica Neue", Arial, sans-serif;
}
```

In this example, the Level 1 title will be displayed in "Helvetica Neue" font if available, otherwise Arial and sans-serif fonts will be used as fallback.

Use custom fonts: You can use custom fonts downloaded or imported from font services like Google Fonts. Follow the instructions provided by the font service to include the font in your HTML document, then use the specific font name in your CSS rule.

```
h2 {
  font-family: "Open Sans", sans-serif;
}
```

In this example, the Level 2 title will appear in the "Open Sans" font if it has been included correctly in the document, otherwise a sans-serif fallback font will be used.

Text sizes and styles

In CSS, you can control text sizes and styles using several properties.

Font size (font-size): This property controls the font size of the text. You can specify a value in pixels, em, rem or percentage.

```
p {
  font-size: 16px;
}
```

Text color (color): This property controls the color of the text. You can specify a value in various formats, such as a color name, hexadecimal code, or RGB value.

```
p {
  color: #333;
}
```

Text style (font-weight, font-style, text-decoration): You can change the text style using these properties. font-weight controls the weight of the font (such as regular, bold, etc.), font-style controls the style of the font (such as regular, italic, etc.), and text-decoration controls the decoration of the text (such as underline, strikethrough , etc.).

```
p {
  font-weight: bold;
  font-style: italic;
  text-decoration: underline;
}
```

These are just a few examples of how you can manage text sizes and styles in CSS. You can experiment with these properties and values to get the look you want for your text.

Spacing and alignment

You can control text spacing and alignment using several properties. Here are some examples:

padding: The property *padding* defines the space between an element's content and its border.

```
div {
  padding: 10px;
}
```

margin: The property *margin* defines the outer space around an element, creating a space between adjacent elements.

```
p {
  margin: 20px;
}
```

text-align: The property *text-align* aligns text within an element horizontally. It can take values such as "left", "right", "center" or "justify".

```
h1 {
  text-align: center;
}
```

line-height: The property *line-height* controls the text line height, i.e. the vertical space between lines.

```
p {
  line-height: 1.5;
}
```

vertical-align: The property *vertical-align* controls the vertical alignment of text within an inline element or table cell.

```
span {
  vertical-align: middle;
}
```

display and **margin: auto**: You can use the combination of *display: flex* and *margin: auto* to center an element horizontally and vertically within its container.

```
.container {
  display: flex;
  justify-content: center; /* Center horizontally */
  align-items: center; /* Center vertically */
}
```

Inheritance of typographic properties

In CSS, many typographic properties are inherited by child elements from their parent elements. This means that if a parent element has a certain typographic property set, child elements will usually inherit that property unless explicitly overridden. Here are some examples of typographic properties that are inherited:

- **font-family**: The font family specified on the parent element is inherited by the child elements.

- **font-size**: The font size set on the parent element is inherited by the child elements.

- **font-weight**: The font weight set on the parent element is inherited by the child elements.

- **font-style**: The font style set on the parent element is inherited by the child elements.

- **color**: The text color set on the parent element is inherited by the child elements.

- **line-height**: Line height set on parent element is inherited by child elements.

However, there are also some typographic properties that are not automatically inherited, such as text-decoration, text-transform and text-align. These properties require that they be explicitly set on each child element if you want to override the parent's default.

It is important to note that inheritance of typographic properties can be affected by other CSS rules specified on child classes or elements. If specific rules are applied to a child element that override the parent's properties, inheritance may not occur as expected.

When creating a typographic layout, it is helpful to consider the inheritance of typographic properties and plan accordingly the structure of the HTML markup and CSS rules to achieve the desired look throughout the document.

Advanced text styles and decorations

Text colors and gradients

You can define text colors using different properties and use gradients to create interesting visual effects. Here are some examples of how you can work with text colors and gradients:

color: The property *color* is used to define the color of text within an element. You can specify the color using the color name, hexadecimal code or RGB value.

```
p {
  color: red;
}
```

Text shades (linear-gradient): You can create color gradients for text using the value *linear-gradient* in the background property and applying it to the containing element.

```
h1 {
  background: linear-gradient(to right, red, blue);
  -webkit-background-clip: text; /* For WebKit browser support */
  -webkit-text-fill-color: transparent; /* For WebKit browser support */
}
```

Text shades (text-fill-color): If you want to apply a color gradient directly to the text without feathering the entire element, you can use the properties *background* and *text-fill-color* Together.

```
h1 {
  background: linear-gradient(to right, red, blue);
  -webkit-background-clip: text; /* For WebKit browser support */
  -webkit-text-fill-color: transparent; /* For WebKit browser support*/
}
```

Gradient effect with shadow (text-shadow): You can create a gradient effect on text using the property *text-shadow* and specifying different colors.

```
h1 {
  text-shadow: 2px 2px 4px rgba(255, 0, 0, 0.5), -2px -2px 4px rgba(0, 0, 255, 0.5);
}
```

Underlines and lines through text

You can add underlines and lines through text using several properties.

Underline (text-decoration): The property *text-decoration* allows you to add an underline to text. You can use the value *underline* to add a standard underline.

```
p {
  text-decoration: underline;
}
```

Line through text (text-decoration): You can use the value *line-through* of the property *text-decoration* to add a line through the text.

```
h1 {
  text-decoration: line-through;
}
```

Personalized line (text-decoration-line): The property *text-decoration-line* allows you to specify the type of line to use for underlines or lines through text. You can use values like *underline* (underline), *line-through* (line across) or *overline* (line above).

```
a {
  text-decoration-line: underline;
}

h1 {
  text-decoration-line: line-through;
}
```

Line color (text-decoration-color): You can specify a custom color for the underline or line through the text using the property *text-decoration-color*.

```
a {
  text-decoration: underline;
  text-decoration-color: red;
}
```

Line style (text-decoration-style): The property *text-decoration-style* allows you to set a custom style for the underline or line through the text. You can use values like *solid* (continuous line), *dashed* (dashed line) or *dotted* (dotted line).

```
p {
  text-decoration: underline;
  text-decoration-style: dashed;
}
```

Special text effects

In CSS, you can create various special effects for text using different properties and techniques. Here are some examples of special text effects:

Text shadow (text-shadow): The *text-shadow* property allows you to add a shadow to text. You can specify the horizontal and vertical position of the shadow and the color of the shadow.

```
h1 {
  text-shadow: 2px 2px 4px rgba(0, 0, 0, 0.5);
}
```

Gradient text (background-clip and text-fill-color): You can create a gradient text effect using the property *background-clip* together with the property *-webkit-text-fill-color*. This only works with WebKit browsers like Chrome and Safari.

```
h1 {
  background: linear-gradient(to right, red, blue);
  -webkit-background-clip: text;
  -webkit-text-fill-color: transparent;
}
```

Text with outline (-webkit-text-stroke): You can create an outline text effect using the property *-webkit-text-stroke*. This only works with WebKit browsers like Chrome and Safari.

```
h1 {
  -webkit-text-stroke: 2px black;
  -webkit-text-fill-color: white;
}
```

Animated text (@keyframes and animation): You can create animation effects on text using rules *@keyframes* and *animation*. You can define animation steps and apply them to text.

```
@keyframes blink {
  0% {
    color: red;
  }
  50% {
    color: blue;
  }
  100% {
    color: red;
  }
}

h1 {
```

```
  animation: blink 1s infinite;
}
```

Text with transparent background (mix-blend-mode): You can apply a color blending effect between the text and the background using the property *mix-blend-mode*. This allows you to create transparent text effects.

```
h1 {
  background-color: black;
  color: white;
  mix-blend-mode: difference;
}
```

Text transformations and transitions

You can apply transformations and transitions to text to create dynamic, animated effects. Here are some examples of how you can use text transformations and transitions.

Transformations (transform): The property *transform* lets you apply different transformations to text, such as rotate, scale, skew, and more.

```
h1 {
  transform: rotate(45deg);
}
```

Transitions (transition): You can create smooth transition effects on text using the property *transition*. This allows you to specify the duration and transition function for a smooth transition between text states.

```
h1 {
  transition: color 0.5s ease-in-out;
}

h1:hover {
  color: red;
}
```

Animations (@keyframes and animation): You can create complex animations on text using rules *@keyframes* and *animation*. You can define animation steps and apply them to text.

```
@keyframes slide-in {
  0% {
   transform: translateX(-100%);
  }
  100% {
   transform: translateX(0);
  }
```

```
}
h1 {
  animation: slide-in 1s ease-in-out;
}
```

3D transformations (transform-style and perspective): You can apply 3D transformations to text using the property *transform-style* and *perspective*. This allows you to create effects of depth and perspective.

```
h1 {
  transform-style: preserve-3d;
  perspective: 1000px;
  transform: rotateY(45deg);
}
```

Use of colors

Background colors

In CSS, you can define the background color of an element using the background-color property. Here are some examples of how you can work with background colors:

Solid color:

```css
body {
  background-color: #f1f1f1;
}

div {
  background-color: rgb(255, 0, 0);
}

span {
  background-color: hsl(120, 50%, 50%);
}
```

Wallpaper \ Background image:

```css
div {
  background-image: url('path/to/image.jpg');
  background-repeat: no-repeat;
  background-size: cover;
}

body {
  background-image: linear-gradient(to right, #ff0000, #00ff00);
}
```

Transparent background:

```css
div {
  background-color: rgba(255, 0, 0, 0.5);
}

h1 {
  background-color: transparent;
}
```

Background with gradients:

```
div {
  background-image: linear-gradient(to right, #ff0000, #00ff00);
}

body {
  background-image: radial-gradient(circle, #ff0000, #00ff00);
}
```

Repeating background:

```
div {
  background-image: url('path/to/image.jpg');
  background-repeat: repeat;
}

body {
  background-image: url('path/to/pattern.png');
  background-repeat: repeat-x;
}
```

Text colors

You can define the text color using the color property. Here are some examples of how you can work with text colors.

Solid color:

```
h1 {
  color: #ff0000;
}

p {
  color: rgb(0, 128, 255);
}

span {
  color: hsl(120, 50%, 50%);
}
```

Text transparency:

```
h1 {
  color: rgba(255, 0, 0, 0.5);
}
```

```
p {
  color: transparent;
}
```

Text color with gradients:

```
h1 {
  background-image: linear-gradient(to right, #ff0000, #00ff00);
  -webkit-background-clip: text;
  -webkit-text-fill-color: transparent;
}
```

Color mixing effects:

```
h1 {
  color: white;
  background-color: black;
  mix-blend-mode: difference;
}
```

Text color with animation:

```
@keyframes color-change {
  0% {
    color: red;
  }
  50% {
    color: blue;
  }
  100% {
    color: red;
  }
}

h1 {
  animation: color-change 1s infinite;
}
```

Transparency and opacity

You can manage the transparency and opacity of an element using various properties. Here are some of the main ones:

Opacity (opacity): The property *opacity* lets you adjust the opacity of an element, from 0 (completely transparent) to 1 (completely opaque).

```
div {
  opacity: 0.5;
}
```

Color with transparency (rgba()): You can use the notation *rgba()* to specify a color with a transparency value. Red (R), green (G), blue (B) values range from 0 to 255 while alpha (A) valid values range from 0 to 1, where 0 represents complete transparency (the color is not visible) and 1 represents full opacity (color is fully visible).

```
h1 {
  color: rgba(255, 0, 0, 0.5);
}
```

Background with transparency:

```
div {
  background-color: rgba(0, 0, 255, 0.3);
}
```

Transparency with gradients (linear-gradient() and radial-gradient()): You can create gradients with transparency using functions *linear-gradient()* and r*adial-gradient()*, combining color values with alpha (transparency).

```
div {
  background-image: linear-gradient(to right, rgba(255, 0, 0, 0.5), rgba(0, 255, 0, 0.5));
}
```

Color mixing effects (mix-blend-mode): The property *mix-blend-mode* allows you to apply color mixing effects, including transparency, between an element and its parent or sibling elements.

```
h1 {
  color: white;
  background-color: black;
  mix-blend-mode: difference;
}
```

Backgrounds and gradients

Solid backgrounds and background images

You can define both solid backgrounds and background images for your page elements. Here's how you can do it:

Solid background (background-color):
You can define a solid background color using the property *background-color*. You can use color values such as predefined color names, hexadecimal codes or functions like rgb() or hsl(). An example follows.

```
body {
  background color: #f1f1f1; /* Hexadecimal color */
}

div {
  background-color: rgb(255, 0, 0); /* RGB value */
}

span {
  background-color: hsl(120, 50%, 50%); /* HSL value */
}
```

Wallpaper \ Background image (background-image):
You can set a background image using the property *background-image*. You can specify a path to the image using the image URL. Example:

```
div {
  background-image: url('path/to/image.jpg');
}
```

You can also control how the background image repeats using the property *background-repeat* and adjust the size of the background image with *background-size*. Below is an example.

```
div {
  background-image: url('path/to/image.jpg');
  background-repeat: no-repeat; /* Don't repeat the image */
  background size: cover; /* Fit the image to cover the entire element */
}
```

Linear and radial gradients

You can create linear and radial gradient backgrounds using the linear-gradient() and radial-gradient() functions.

Linear gradients:
You can create linear gradients by specifying the direction of the gradient and the start and end colors. You can also add more colors to create more complex gradients.
Example of a horizontal linear gradient from left to right:

```
div {
  background-image: linear-gradient(to right, #ff0000, #00ff00);
}
```

Example of a diagonal linear gradient:

```
div {
  background-image: linear-gradient(to bottom right, #ff0000, #00ff00);
}
```

Radial gradients:
You can create radial gradients by specifying the starting point and ending point of the gradient. You can define the shape type of the gradient, such as circle or ellipse, and add intermediate colors to create more complex effects.
Example of a radial gradient from one color to another:

```
div {
  background-image: radial-gradient(circle, #ff0000, #00ff00);
}
```

Example of a radial gradient with intermediate colors:

```
div {
  background-image: radial-gradient(circle, #ff0000, #ff8000, #00ff00);
}
```

You can experiment with starting and ending points, shapes and colors to create your own unique gradients. The linear-gradient() and radial-gradient() functions offer many creative possibilities for creating eye-catching backgrounds in your design.

Advanced background effects

In CSS, you can create advanced background effects using different properties and techniques.

Striped background:
You can create a striped background using alternating linear gradients with different colors. Specifies the direction of the gradient to create horizontal or vertical lines.

```
div {
  background-image: linear-gradient(to right, #f9f9f9 50%, #ffffff 50%);
  background-size: 200% 100%;
  background-position: right;
}
```

Polka dot background:
You can create a polka dot background using alternating radial gradients with different colors. You can adjust the size of the polka dots by varying the radius of the gradient.

```
div {
  background-image: radial-gradient(circle, #f9f9f9 20%, transparent 20%);
  background-size: 10px 10px;
}
```

Blurred background effect:
You can apply a blurry background using the blur filter. You can specify the blur value to adjust the intensity of blur.

```
div {
  background-image: url('path/to/image.jpg');
  filter: blur(5px);
}
```

Diagonal striped background effect:
You can create a diagonal striped background using rotated linear gradients.

```
div {
  background-image: linear-gradient(-45deg, #f9f9f9 25%, #ffffff 25%, #ffffff 75%, #f9f9f9 75%);
  background-size: 8px 8px;
}
```

These are just a few examples of advanced background effects you can create in CSS. Experiment with different properties, such as background-image, background-size, background-position, and filters, to get the effects you want in your design.

Borders and frames

Edge properties

Border properties in CSS allow you to customize the look and style of element borders.

border-width: defines the thickness of the border. You can specify a value in pixels, em, rem or percentage. Example:

```
div {
  border-width: 2px;
}
```

border-style: defines the style of the border. You can use values such as solid, dotted, dashed, double, groove, ridge, inset, outset or none. Example:

```
div {
  border-style: dashed;
}
```

border-color: defines the color of the border. You can use predefined color names, hexadecimal codes or functions like rgb() or hsl(). For example:

```
div {
  border-color: #ff0000;
}
```

border: A short form for defining properties at the same time *border-width*, *border-style* and *border-color*. An example follows.

```
div {
  border: 1px solid #000000;
}
```

border-image: allows you to use an image for the border instead of a color. You can specify image URL, repeat, border width and other options. For example:

```
div {
  border-image: url('path/to/image.jpg') 10 10 round;
}
```

Border radius

The border-radius property in CSS is used to round the corners of an element, creating smooth edges. You can define a border-radius value to specify the radius of curvature of the corners.

Single value:
You can specify a value of *border-radius* for all corners of the element. For example, a value of 10px will make all corners have a radius of 10px.

```
div {
  border-radius: 10px;
}
```

Separate values for angles:
You can specify separate values for the element's corners using the syntax [top-left] [top-right] [bottom-right] [bottom-left]. For example, you can set only the top corners with a 10px radius and leave the bottom corners without rounding.

```
div {
  border-radius: 10px 10px 0 0;
}
```

Separate values for horizontal and vertical angles:
You can specify separate values for horizontal (left and right) and vertical (top and bottom) angles using the syntax [horizontal-value] / [vertical-value]. For example, you can set a 10px radius for horizontal corners and a 20px radius for vertical corners.

```
div {
  border-radius: 10px / 20px;
}
```

You can also use percentage values instead of pixels to define the radius of the edges.

```
div {
  border-radius: 50%;
}
```

Box shadow

The box-shadow property in CSS allows you to add shadows to an element. You can use this property to create depth and dimension effects on page elements.

The general syntax for box-shadow is as follows:

```
box-shadow: [horizontal] [vertical] [fading] [diffusion] [color];
```

- **horizontal**: Specifies the horizontal offset of the shadow from the element. A negative value shifts the shadow to the left, while a positive value shifts it to the right. You can use units of measurement such as pixels (px) or percentages (%).

- **vertical**: Specifies the vertical offset of the shadow from the element. A negative value moves the shadow up, while a positive value moves it down. You can use units of measurement such as pixels (px) or percentages (%).

- **fading**: Specifies the intensity of the shadow. A larger value indicates a softer shadow, while a smaller value indicates a sharper shadow. You can use units of measurement such as pixels (px) or percentages (%).

- **spread**: Specifies the dispersion of the shadow. A larger value indicates a more extensive shadow, while a smaller value indicates a more compact shadow. You can use units of measurement such as pixels (px) or percentages (%).

- **color**: Specifies the color of the shadow. You can use predefined color names, hexadecimal codes or functions like rgb() or rgba().

Example of a simple shadow with horizontal and vertical offset:

```
div {
  box-shadow: 3px 3px #000000;
}
```

Example of a shadow with custom horizontal, vertical offset, fade, and diffusion:

```
div {
  box-shadow: 5px 5px 10px 2px #000000;
}
```

You can use the box-shadow property to create different combinations of shadows to get the desired effect. Experiment with different values to create custom shadows and enrich the design of your elements.

Multiple frames

Multi-frames in CSS allow you to apply multiple borders to an element, creating complex and detailed frame effects. You can use the border property to define multiple frames on a single element.

The syntax for defining multiple frames is as follows:

```
border: [width] [style] [color], [width] [style] [color], ...;
```

You can specify multiple frames separated by commas, each with its own width, style and color.

Here is an example of using multiple frames:

```
div {
  border: 2px solid red, 4px dotted blue, 6px dashed green;
}
```

In this example, the div element will have three overlapping frames: a 2-pixel red frame with a solid style, a 4-pixel blue frame with a dot style, and a 6-pixel green frame with a dashed style.

CSS transitions and transformations

State transitions

State transitions refer to the animation of an element when a certain state occurs, such as hovering over or focusing on an element. This state can be defined using pseudo-class selectors such as :hover, :focus or :active. State transitions are applied through the transition property and can animate changes to one or more properties when the state change occurs.

Here is an example of using state transitions:

```
div {
  background-color: red;
  transition: background-color 0.3s ease;
}

div:hover {
  background-color: blue;
}
```

In this example, when the mouse hovers over the button, the background color gradually changes from red to blue over 0.3 seconds.

Property transitions

Property transitions let you animate changes to one or more properties of an element over time, regardless of state. You can specify the properties to animate using the transition property and define the duration, time-function and delay to control the appearance of the animation:

```
transition: [properties] [duration] [time-function] [delay];
```

- **property**: Specify the CSS properties you want to animate during the transition. You can specify a single property or multiple properties separated by commas.

- **duration**: Specifies the duration of the animation in seconds (s) or milliseconds (ms). For example, 0.5s indicates a duration of half a second.

- **time-function**: Specifies the transition function that determines how the animation evolves over time. Some common features include linear (smooth animation), ease (acceleration and deceleration animation), ease-in (acceleration animation), ease-out (deceleration animation), and ease-in-out (acceleration and deceleration animation).

- **delay**: Specifies the delay before the animation starts, in seconds (s) or milliseconds (ms).

Here's an example of using property transitions:

```
div {
  width: 200px;
  background-color: red;
  transition: width 0.3s ease, background-color 0.3s ease;
}

div:hover {
  width: 300px;
  background-color: blue;
}
```

In this case, when the mouse is hovered over the div element, the width expands from 200px to 300px and the background color gradually changes from red to blue in 0.3 seconds.

2D and 3D transformations

2D and 3D transformations in CSS allow you to change the position, size and appearance of elements in two- or three-dimensional space.

The **2D transformations** can be applied using the following CSS properties:

- **transform**: Specifies a 2D transformation for the item, such as rotate, scale, move, and offset.

- **translate**: Moves the element along the X and Y axes relative to its original position.

- **rotate**: Rotates the item around a specified origin point.

- **scale**: Scales the item by specified scale factors.

Here is an example of using 2D transforms:

```
div {
  transform: translate(50px, 50px) rotate(45deg) scale(1.5);
}
```

In this example, the div element will be moved 50 pixels along the X and Y axes, rotated 45 degrees around its point of origin, and scaled 150% from its original size.

The **3D transformations**, on the other hand, allow you to apply transformation effects in a three-dimensional space using the following CSS properties:

- **transform**: Specifies a 3D transformation for the item, such as rotation, scale, displacement, and perspective.

- **translate3d**: Moves the element along the X, Y and Z axes from its original position.

- **rotate3d**: Rotates the item around the X, Y, and Z axes by specified angles.

- **scale3d**: Scales the item by specified scale factors along the X, Y, and Z axes.

Here's an example of using 3D transforms:

```
div {
  transform: translate3d(100px, 100px, 50px) rotate3d(1, 0, 1, 45deg) scale3d(1.5, 1.5, 1.5);
}
```

In this example, the div element will be moved 100 pixels along the X, Y and Z axes, rotated 45 degrees around the X and Z axes, and scaled 150% along the X, Y and Z axes.

CSS animations

Creating animations with keyframes

Creating keyframes animations in CSS allows you to define a series of intermediate stages for animating an element. You can use the rule *@keyframes* to define intermediate stages and specify properties that change during the animation.

The syntax for creating animations with keyframes is as follows:

```
@keyframes animation-name {
  stadium1 {
   /* define properties for stage 1 */
  }
  studio2 {
   /* define properties for stage 2 */
  }
  /* other intermediate stages */
  Stadium {
   /* define properties for stage N */
  }
}
```

Where:

- **animation-name** is a unique name that you give to your animation.

- **stadium1, studio2, Stadium** are custom names that you assign to the intermediate stages of the animation.

- within each stage, you can specify the CSS properties you want to animate.

Here's an example of creating a keyframed animation that rotates an element:

```
@keyframes rotate {
  0% {
   transform: rotate(0deg);
  }
  100% {
   transform: rotate(360deg);
  }
}

div {
  animation-name: rotate;
  animation-duration: 3s;
  animation-timing-function: linear;
```

```
    animation-iteration-count: infinite;
}
```

In this example, an animation called rotate is defined using keyframes. The div element applies the animation using the animation-name property with the name of the animation, animation-duration to specify the duration of the animation (3 seconds), animation-timing-function to specify the timing function of the animation (linear) and animation-iteration-count to specify how many times the animation should repeat (in this case, infinite times).

Timing and animation functions

Here are some of the more common properties used for animations:

- **animation-duration**: Specifies the duration of the animation in a certain time interval. You can specify the value in seconds (s) or milliseconds (ms).

- **animation-delay**: Specifies the delay before an animation starts running. You can specify the value in seconds (s) or milliseconds (ms).

- **animation-timing-function**: Specifies the timing function used to control the speed of the animation. Some common values include linear (constant speed), ease (slow start and fast finish), ease-in (slow start), ease-out (fast finish), and ease-in-out (slow start and fast finish).

- **animation-iteration-count**: Specifies how many times the animation should repeat. You can use a specific number (for example, 2 to repeat twice) or the value infinite to repeat the animation indefinitely.

- **animation-direction**: Specifies the direction in which the animation should run. Some common values include normal (forward), reverse (backward), alternate (forward and reverse), and alternate-reverse (backward and forward).

- **animation-fill-mode**: Specifies the behavior of the element before and after running the animation. Some common values include none (no effect), forwards (keep the final state of the animation), and backwards (apply the initial state of the animation).

- **animation-play-state**: Specifies the playback status of the animation. You can use the value running to start the animation or paused to pause the animation.

You can combine these properties to precisely control the timing and playback of your animations. For example:

```
div {
    animation-name: my-animation;
    animation-duration: 3s;
    animation-timing-function: ease-in-out;
    animation-iteration-count: 2;
    animation-direction: alternate;
    animation-fill-mode: forwards;
```

```
    animation-play-state: running;
}
```

In this example, the animation called my-animation will run for 3 seconds using an "ease-in-out" timing function. It will loop twice, forward and backward, and will keep the final state of the animation after it's played.

Responsive design

Introduction to responsive design

Responsive design is an approach to website design and development that aims to create an optimal user experience across different sizes and devices, such as desktop, tablet, and mobile devices. The main objective of responsive design is to ensure that the content and the arrangement of the elements adapt fluidly and intuitively to the available screen space of the device used by the user.

The importance of responsive design is linked to the growing use of mobile devices to access the web. With a wide range of screen sizes and orientations, it's critical that websites scale and look appropriate on all devices, providing a consistent and accessible browsing experience.

Responsive design uses several techniques and tools, including media queries, layout flexibility, and the use of relative units of measurement, to tailor the appearance and arrangement of elements based on device characteristics. This allows you to resize and rearrange content, adjust text size, scale images, and more, to provide optimal viewing and easy navigation on any screen.

One of the main advantages of responsive design is that it allows you to maintain a single website, rather than having to create separate versions for different devices. This simplifies site management and reduces the need to duplicate content or make multiple changes.

Media queries

CSS media queries allow you to apply specific style rules based on the characteristics of the device used to view the website. This allows you to dynamically adjust the look and layout of your site based on screen size, orientation, resolution, and other device attributes.

The syntax of media queries is as follows:

```
@media media_type and (condition) {
  /* style rules to apply */
}
```

Where "media_type" specifies the type of output device or medium, such as screen (computer, tablet and mobile device screens), print (printouts), speech (text-to-speech), etc.

And "condition" represents the specifications that must be met for the style rules to apply. Conditions can include different attributes such as screen width, screen height, orientation, pixel density, resolution, etc.

Here's an example of a media query that applies a specific style when the screen width is less than 600 pixels:

```
@media screen and (max-width: 600px) {
  /* style rules to apply for screens smaller than 600px */
}
```

In this example, the style rules within the media query will only be applied when the screen width is less than 600 pixels.

Media queries allow you to create responsive designs, where you can define different layouts, sizes, and styles for different screen sizes. You can use multiple media queries with different conditions to tailor the design to meet your specific needs.

For example, you can use media queries to reflow content, adjust text size, hide or show elements, change alignment, and more, based on screen size.

Optimization of the CSS code

Code consolidation and reduction

CSS code consolidation and minification are techniques used to improve the efficiency and maintainability of your code. This process involves reviewing and optimizing existing CSS code to make it more compact, organized, and readable.

Here are some tips for consolidating and reducing your CSS code:

- **Delete unused code**: Remove any CSS rules that are no longer needed in your project. This will reduce the size of your CSS file and make it easier to maintain.

- **Combine and reduce selectors**: Try to combine similar selectors and apply the same rules to multiple elements. This will reduce the amount of repetitive code and simplify future changes.

- **Use abbreviations and shorthands**: Take advantage of abbreviations and CSS shorthand syntax to reduce the amount of code. For example, you can use margin: 0 instead of specifying margin-top: 0, margin-right: 0, margin-bottom: 0 and margin-left: 0 separately.

- **Use CSS variables**: CSS variables, defined with --variable-name, allow you to store and reuse common values. This makes it easy to keep the design up to date and consistent across your project.

- **Group similar rules**: If you have similar CSS rules, you can group them together by separating them with commas. For example, instead of having separate rules for .class1, .class2, .class3, you can group them as .class1, .class2, .class3 { ... }.

- **Use CSS libraries**: CSS libraries like Bootstrap or Tailwind CSS offer predefined classes that can be used for common styles. This can reduce the amount of CSS code you have to write manually.

- **Minify the CSS code**: Use CSS minification or compression tools to reduce whitespace, comments and extra lines in your code. This will make your CSS file lighter and improve your website loading times.

- **Organize your code**: Use a consistent organization structure in your CSS file, using comments or sections to separate different pieces of code. This will make your code more readable and easier to navigate.

Shrinking and consolidating your CSS code can improve your website's performance, make it easier to maintain, and ensure cleaner, more manageable code over time.

Compression and minification tools

There are several tools available for compressing and minifying CSS code. These tools reduce the size of CSS files by removing blank spaces, comments, and other unnecessary information, thereby improving the loading performance of your website. Here are some popular tools for compressing and minifying CSS code:

- **CSSNano**: CSSNano is a CSS compression tool that uses several techniques to reduce CSS file size, such as removing whitespace, compressing colors, and simplifying selectors. It can be used via command line or as part of an automation workflow.

- **UglifyCSS**: UglifyCSS is another CSS code compression and minification tool. Remove blank spaces, comments and reduce the size of CSS rules to improve the performance of your website.

- **CleanCSS**: CleanCSS is a CSS code cleanup and optimization tool. In addition to compression, it also offers features such as optimizing colors, removing redundant declarations, and simplifying CSS selectors.

- **PostCSS**: PostCSS is a modular framework that allows you to perform different transformations on your CSS code. You can use specific plugins, such as cssnano or autoprefixer, for compressing and optimizing your CSS code.

- **Online CSS Minifier**: There are several free online tools that allow you to load and minify CSS code right in your browser, without the need to install any software. These tools offer a quick option to reduce the size of your CSS code without having to set up a separate development environment.

Performance and cache

Website performance is a key aspect of providing a good user experience. One of the factors affecting performance is the browser cache, which stores website files on the user's device to reduce the loading time of subsequent pages. In the context of CSS, caching can be leveraged to optimize the performance of your website. Here are some strategies to optimize the cache and improve the performance of your CSS code:

- **Use an appropriate versioning strategy**: When making changes to your CSS file, be sure to change the URL of the CSS file or use a query parameter to force the browser to download the updated version. This way, the browser will detect that the file has been changed and update the cache.

- **Set a proper cache expiration**: Configure the Cache-Control HTTP header on your server to specify how long the CSS file should be cached in the browser. You can set a value like max-age to specify the cache age in seconds.

- **Minify the CSS code**: Reduce the size of your CSS file by using compression and minification tools, like the ones mentioned earlier. A smaller CSS file size will reduce download time and contribute to faster performance.

- **Use file concatenation**: If possible, bundle several CSS files into one to reduce the number of HTTP requests to the server. Concatenation will reduce overall CSS download time and allow for better caching management.

- **Use server caching**: Configure your web server to allow CSS file caching. You can do this through the use of HTTP headers like Expires or Cache-Control, which tell the browser how long to cache the file.

- **Leverage content delivery network (CDN) caching**: If you are using a CDN to serve your CSS files, make sure the CDN is configured to use caching and set the HTTP headers correctly to optimize caching.

- **Avoid using dynamic URLs**: Avoid using URLs with dynamic parameters for CSS files. This may cause the browser to fail to cache due to changing the URL with each request.

Optimizing your browser cache for your CSS code will help improve the performance of your website, reducing page load time and providing a faster user experience. Be sure to test and monitor your website performance using analytics tools to check the effectiveness of your optimizations.

Browser compatibility and fallback

Browser support and vendor prefixes

Browser support and vendor prefixes are two important aspects to consider when writing CSS code to ensure that your website works well across different platforms and browsers. Here is a brief explanation of both:

Browser support: Modern browsers support a wide range of CSS features, but there may be some differences in the implementation of certain CSS properties or new features. It is important to check the compatibility of your CSS code with the most common browsers, such as Google Chrome, Mozilla Firefox, Safari and Microsoft Edge.

You can refer to websites like "Can I use" (https://caniuse.com/) to check browser support for different CSS properties. These sites provide detailed information on the level of browser support for each property, including legacy browsers. If a particular property is not supported by a particular browser, you may need to find alternatives or fallback solutions.

Prefix vendor: Vendor prefixes are prefixes added to CSS property names to indicate that that specific feature is still experimental or is only supported by a particular browser or rendering engine. For example, to take advantage of CSS3 features in some browsers, you might need to use prefixes like -webkit- for Safari and Chrome, -moz- for Firefox, -o- for Opera, and -ms- for Internet Explorer.

Using vendor prefixes can be useful for testing new CSS features in preview, but it's important to note that they shouldn't be used as a long-term solution. As CSS features become stable and supported by browsers without the use of prefixes, it is recommended that you update your code and remove unnecessary prefixes.

However, with the advent of more up-to-date modern browsers, the use of vendor prefixes is becoming less common. We recommend that you check browser compatibility and use prefixes only when absolutely necessary, trying to provide a consistent experience across all supported browsers.

Finally, it's a good practice to test your website on a variety of browsers and versions to ensure that your CSS code works well and offers a good user experience on all devices.

Fallback for unsupported features

When using advanced CSS features or properties that may not be supported by all browsers, it's important to provide a fallback or alternative to ensure a consistent experience for users visiting your website on older or unsupported browsers. Here are some common approaches to handle fallbacks for unsupported features:

- **Using standard CSS properties**: If the advanced feature you're using has a corresponding standard CSS property that offers similar behavior, you can use that as a fallback. For example, if you're using flexbox for layout, you can provide a float-based alternative or display:table for browsers that don't support flexbox.

- **Media queries:** You can use media queries to apply different styles based on screen size or browser-supported features. For example, you can apply a grid layout only for larger screen sizes, while using a float or inline-block based alternative for smaller devices.

- **JavaScript**: In some cases, you may need to use JavaScript to handle fallbacks. You can detect unsupported features via JavaScript and apply alternative styles or behaviors accordingly. For example, you can use a JavaScript library like Modernizr to detect support for specific features and apply styles or layout choices based on this detection.

- **Warning messages**: If an unsupported feature doesn't have a direct fallback alternative, you can provide a warning message to users using unsupported browsers, encouraging them to upgrade their browser or use a modern browser for a better experience. You can do this by using JavaScript or by providing a static message within your HTML markup.

It's important to test the fallbacks carefully to make sure they work properly and provide the right experience on all supported devices and browsers. Test your website on different browsers and versions, including older ones, to ensure that fallbacks are implemented correctly and that your website is accessible to a wide range of users.

Backwards compatibility techniques

When it comes to making your CSS code backwards compatible, there are several techniques you can use to make your website work properly even in older or less modern browsers. Here are some of the common techniques:

- **Progressive enhancement**: This technique is based on the concept of providing a basic working experience for all users and then progressively improving it for those who use more modern browsers or support advanced features. Basically, you start with a CSS codebase that works on older browsers and add styles and advanced features only if they're supported.

- **Graceful degradation**: This technique is the opposite of progressive enhancement. We start with a high-end experience using advanced features, but provide a simpler alternative for older or unsupported browsers. Basically, it initially develops for modern browsers, then tests and provides fallback for unsupported features.

- **Polyfills**: A polyfill is a piece of JavaScript code that fills functionality gaps in browsers. You can use polyfills to provide support for unsupported CSS features, like flexbox or grid. Polyfills detect if a feature isn't supported and apply the JavaScript code needed to reproduce or emulate it.

- **CSS Reset**: A CSS reset is a snippet of code that removes browsers' default styles and provides a common foundation on which to build your layout. This helps ensure greater consistency across browsers and avoid significant differences in how your items look across different platforms.

- **Browser-specific CSS**: In some cases, you may need to use specific CSS rules for a particular browser or version. This can be done using vendor prefixes or by specifying alternate styles within browser-specific media queries. However, it's important to use this technique sparingly and only when necessary, trying to keep your code as clean and readable as possible.

- **Testing on different browsers and devices**: It is crucial to test your website on a wide variety of browsers and devices to check for backwards compatibility. Use emulators or real devices to test your site on older or less common browsers and check that everything works fine.

In general, it is advisable to follow web development guidelines and CSS specifications to ensure the greatest possible compatibility. Keep your code clean, modular, and well organized, so you can easily make changes or fixes if needed

Framework CSS

Introduction to CSS frameworks

A CSS framework is a predefined set of styles, components, and tools that simplify web development by providing a solid foundation for building websites or applications. CSS frameworks are designed to speed up the development process by providing a consistent style, organized structure, and built-in functionality.

Here are some benefits of using a CSS framework:

- **Time saving**: CSS frameworks provide pre-built components, such as grids, forms, buttons, navbars, and more, that can be easily used in your project without having to write them from scratch. This allows you to save time and focus more on developing your content or specific features.

- **Consistent style**: CSS frameworks offer a consistent, predefined style that can be applied to all components of your website. This ensures that your elements fit together well, regardless of their position on the page. Additionally, frameworks often follow design and usability best practices, ensuring a good user experience.

- **Responsiveness**: Many CSS frameworks are designed to create layouts that are responsive and adaptable to different screen sizes. Responsive grids make it easy to organize and position your elements on the page, making sure your website looks good on mobile, tablet and desktop devices.

- **Multi-browser support**: CSS frameworks are tested on different browsers and versions to ensure good cross-browser compatibility. This allows you to develop your website with the confidence that it will work well on a range of platforms.

- **Community and resources**: CSS frameworks usually have a large community of developers actively using and supporting them. This means you can find plenty of resources, documentation, tutorials, and support forums that will help you learn and use the framework effectively.

Some examples of popular CSS frameworks include Bootstrap, Foundation, Bulma and Tailwind CSS. Each of them has its own characteristics, styles and methods of use, so it is advisable to examine their documentation to understand which one best suits your needs.

However, it's important to note that using a CSS framework isn't always necessary. Whether you have unique design needs or prefer to write your own custom CSS, you can always create your own style without using a framework. Whether or not to use a framework depends on the specific needs of your project and your comfort level with CSS.

Using popular frameworks

Using popular frameworks can streamline the web development process by offering a set of pre-built components and tools. Here's a quick rundown on how to use two of the most popular CSS frameworks: Bootstrap and Tailwind CSS.

Bootstrap:

- **Installation**: You can install Bootstrap into your project in several ways, such as using CSS and JavaScript files downloaded from the official site or using a package manager like npm. Follow the Bootstrap documentation for detailed installation instructions.

- **Integration**: Once Bootstrap is installed, you can integrate it into your project by including CSS and JavaScript files in your HTML pages. You can do this using <link> tags for CSS and <script> for JavaScript. Be sure to also include the jQuery dependency if you intend to use Bootstrap interactive components that require it.

- **Use of components**: Bootstrap provides a wide range of pre-built components such as grids, forms, buttons, navbars, carousels and many more. You can use these components by adding the appropriate CSS classes to HTML elements. See the Bootstrap documentation for examples and details on how to use specific components.

- **Personalization**: Bootstrap offers customization options that allow you to tailor the framework to your needs. You can customize the CSS variables or use the Sass version of Bootstrap to easily change the style of the components.

Tailwind CSS:

- **Installation**: To use Tailwind CSS, you need to install it in your project. You can do this by using npm or yarn as package managers. Follow the instructions in the Tailwind CSS documentation for proper installation.

- **Configuration**: After installation, you will need to create a tailwind.config.js configuration file in your project. This file allows you to customize Tailwind CSS settings, such as colors, fonts, and other variables. You can also enable or disable specific components according to your needs.

- **Using classes**: Tailwind CSS relies on using atomic classes to style elements. Tailwind's classes are based on utility classes that you can apply directly to HTML elements. For example, you can use the bg-blue-500 class to set the background color to blue. The Tailwind CSS documentation provides a complete list of available classes and their meanings.

- **Personalization**: Although Tailwind CSS offers a set of predefined classes, you can easily customize the framework to fit your design. You can edit the configuration variables in the tailwind.config.js file to customize colors, sizes, margins, and more.

Remember that both Bootstrap and Tailwind CSS offer many more features and options that can be explored through their respective documentations. The choice of framework depends on your personal preferences, project needs, and the functionality you're looking for.

Outro

Throughout this how-to guide, we've explored the fundamentals and advanced techniques of CSS, giving you a solid foundation for creating compelling styles and dynamic layouts for your web projects. We've covered concepts like selectors, box models, flexible layouts, animations, media queries, and much more. We hope you found this guide helpful in understanding and mastering CSS.

Remember that CSS is a powerful tool that allows you to customize the look and layout of your web pages in creative ways. Keep experimenting, exploring new features, and following the latest CSS developments to stay up-to-date on industry best practices and trends.

With the knowledge gained, you will be able to turn your ideas into digital reality, creating beautiful and functional websites. Let your creative side express itself through the design and arrangement of elements, making the most of the potential of CSS.

We hope that "Easy CSS - Handy Guide" has provided you with a solid foundation of knowledge and inspired you to delve further into the wonderful world of CSS. Whether you're a beginner or an expert, we're sure you'll continue to improve your skills and create stunning designs using CSS.

Have a good journey in your learning trip and in the exploration of the infinite potential of the web!

www.ingramcontent.com/pod-product-compliance
Lightning Source LLC
LaVergne TN
LVHW081532050326
832903LV00025B/1756